these memories require

First published 2025 by

Puncher and Wattmann

puncherandwattmann.com

Individual poetry collection by Jacinta Le Plastrier (c. 2025)
This book is copyright. Aside from fair dealing for the purposes of study,
research, criticism, review, or as otherwise permitted under the Copyright
Act, no part may be reproduced by any process without written permission.
Inquiries should be addressed to the publisher.
Publication date: 1 March 2025

National Library of Australia

Cataloguing-in-Publication data:

these memories require

ISBN: 978-0-9923189-2-5

70 pp / Typeset in Georgia

Cover and Design: Sophie Gaur
Cover image: Photocollage, Primary image credit: Midjourney v 6.2.
Response to "Grainy image of an old empty room with a door half open,
peeling wallpaper" AI-generated image. Midjourney Inc, Nov 11th, 2024.

Printed by Lightning Source International

Jacinta Le Plastrier

these memories require

PUNCHER & WATTMANN

In publishing these poems I have been committed to an ethical practice where I do not identify directly another's experience, without explicit permissions being in place. In regard to Federico Lorca and Walter Benjamin, their histories are public and substantiated.

The poems in this book have been conceived upon, or written about or on, places which are unceded lands in so called Australia. In this book these include the lands of the first peoples of the Yorta Yorta, the Arrernte, the Wathaurong, the Bundjalung, the Gunaikurnai, the Gulidjan and Gadubanud, the Djab Wurrung and most specifically, I live, write and work on the countries of the Boon Wurrung and the Wurundjeri Woi Wurrung. I pay my deepest respects to these lands' elders, poets and communities. I acknowledge the continuing suffering and suppression of human rights for Australian First Nations persons and persons of other nations.

for my daughters
Saskia, Coco & Bebe

untitled (Kill,)	1
returnings	2
construction site	4
impossible	5
untitled (dolls)	7
secret	8
untitled (o,)	9
By which you mean,	10
untitled (later)	11
untitled (the children)	12
untitled (perhaps)	13
Plainsong (for c.)	14
icu (for b.)	15
quartet (for s.)	17
neuroward2east (for a.b.)	21
unnamed	22
untitled (once)	24

II

prologue	27
untitled (witchly)	28
untitled (i want)	29
amendment	30
untitled (did i)	31
untitled (recovery)	32
untitled (On)	34
untitled (the earth lugs on)	36
untitled (when)	37
pollination	38
untitled (time)	39
the storm	40
untitled (ahoy)	42
untitled (jump)	46
Catalogue	47
untitled (pacing)	50
Canto 1	52
untitled (nascent)	54
in the sea's	55
untitled (long)	56
End-notes	58
Acknowledgements	59

untitled (Kill,)

the assassin
or be kill'd

love can be Fascist. For many reasons, you h've watch'd

over and over again,
   Bertolucci's Masterpiece, *Il Conformista*. The Conformist. (1970)

in it, dear Reader, look it up!
the protagonist male will repeatedly, to save
their skinny skin, turncoat, change colours
to the victorious one

over and over, in the cinema of your mind, you see her
   betrayed
   fled through the snow, the forest, all those trees
   until she has been finally tracked, stunned, sniper'd & stupefied.
   lies blooded, in stockings and furs

returnings

notbirthhouse, not juvenility's home,
        but the dwelling you habitually
            return to

in sleep's dreams. how often
        you find yourself there!
            wandering, in slumber's

reconnaissance, the stupefied
        ether
            of the somnambulist.

it is true
        the storeys, shapes
            of its rooms, configurations

alter
        in phantasm's shadows.
            and you are nearly

always like a child,
        both within yourself, and yet
            with your own gaze,

you are able
        to watch you.
            nightgown dressed,

you float, spectral
        through its doors,
                across thresholds.

but this was a house
        in which you also lived,
                really,

for many years. it was the house
        that taught you
                how to write

construction site

i am not talking of the wall's scream, how it screamed
      so whitely,
how every chair turned away,
how every thread, that anchored each stone
      in me, snapped

i had lost my way earlier.
      and the beauty hurt,
of the city belly unearthed
      like that, history
rupturing outwards

then pared back
      into pillars, huge teeth
lodged. i wanted to climb
      the rubble,

hold a single stone.
let its weight convince me,
      my eye was a hand

impossible

impossible to say
why we cannot, always
be attentive
to what only matters.
the tendrils that spin
the heart-cage.
                        in dawn's silt
those who are lovers do.
            eyes lidded, they rock
            in the bay
            which evades time—

why you, only,
in the auditoria of strangers,
do i lay beside?
there is another way,
a brute coinage, exchanges
enforced for favours—

but we wrack
to the bone instead,
as it is needed.
to reach, each, back
from the brinks of dissolutions.

to allow the deaths cyclical, of selves,
which can be substantial.

    also, the inflorescence
    that roots in the carcasses
    of these losses.
together rare, yes
but with cost,
    the brandings by
    the sustaining of determination.
    never to surrender
    the other up

untitled (dolls)

all witches
have dolls.
yours at five
years old. you
savage her
with scissors,
hair cut
so she resembles
a salem accused; break
both plastic arms;
abandon her
in the field
right next
to your home

secret

there was a boy in the woods
a boy in the lane. Which boy?
We can't remember

A face in the woods a face in the lane
What was the name What was the name

We can't remember. You must remember
You will never remember

untitled (o,)

o, Child

who sprang

open-armed, over

the tall, rusted

athletic hurdle.

The bush-school's

yard, slanted

steeply, gravelled.

Scabs, hard as rubies.

By which you mean,

there are corrosions

that heal yet mark.

The small frond of a scar

from childhood's kneecap.

And of those lances, rarer

whose wound is not bared

on the physical

but devour, scalpel

invisible, deepest?

Whether inlaid

by self's treachery

or that of others.

The soul's mouth, even

can still not form the words

which might shield them

untitled (later)

later,

the children will quieten,

and the clear silence culled

from the feet of their laughter

will lower into rooms

where shadowed

children dream.

of dolls vagrant,

their clotted hair.

marbles splashing

on ashen floors.

and of the unicorns

who slink, behind

the brunt of dawn,

exiled by reason

untitled (the children)

the children chase

the glinting air,

swift with bubbles.

their opalescences

perfectly sphered.

in skins, thinned.

mouths blow miracles

which flee

untitled (perhaps)

perhaps you thought
i was a god—

how i glittered
through courses

of mud—how pure
my mercy was

—& how i would open
my garnet mouth.

but be
assured

—i shook
every moment.

Plainsong (for c.)

her lot is terrible, premature losses
   she has been practising to turn upon
she is marked, as some are, and innocently
   by precocity: has audible speech
early, take in almost casually the secrets
   of music, cello, bass, piano, guitar
harmonica and accordion and voice.
   of late, at sixteen, the ukelele

also the alchemy of the words of songs
   she makes in composing to be her own
grief's ionisation into a survival
   a search-lighting for beauty, joy's glitching.
her insistence on hauling darkness in
   for its precious illumination

icu (for b.)

born unbreathing blue
yanked you

to touch you
only through

glassy slits,
you gloved gravely

into
incubator.

in the errata
of shock

the room's light
is also eerily electrically

blued,
as in the depths of a vast aquarium

you essential
as shell, husk

immaculately small
cored

by tubes, sharpnesses
at the inner wrist, nasal—

g. dies in the glasscot
exactly next to you,
her parents' grief
at 3 am, at the royal women's hospital, total.

machines
lung you

bruise you
with their marvels, prodigal

quartet (for s.)

who is getting it wrong?
you, dear first child
or the specialists helpful with their rules.
in every photograph of childhood you glow

feyly lustrous, healthful
with by my young-mother love for you—
carted you all around, sidekick
to work and university

piggied you up that long shale cliff
in the MacDonnell Ranges east of Alice/Mparntwe too,
who lived all alone with you,
hope fierce and candid and daily

i almost failed you,
almost let-in their slurs
which whispered—chronically,
underlit like radium your sleeping.

    *

for sure, in adulthood, some of your letters
habitually reverse, *esipode* for episode
or you cannibalise a term, *Kringle* for Kindle
on which you read obsessively
the priveted dreams of books.
and your phone's voice message
has an elocution careful

a manner, old-fashioned in its politesse,
the scour of years of speech pathology
by which you reformed your sounds.
you explored the manipulation
of tongue, sensed it
against the tissue of mouth-roof, floor and jaw.
a skill the naturally articulate
may never be arrested to learn.
you scouted the typography of the vocable—
consonants, some gentle some hard—
the required gymnastics of the uh-ee-oh of vowels.
there were specialists for sight,
hearing, the lack of diction
in your heavy limbs, but not for all the things:
all invited in the class
to a birthday party except for you.
you didn't run
in the school athletics carnival,
you skipped along,
lag the 100-metre sprint-field by 70,
unsure of direction
to the finishing line, it seemed
bewildered by where you were going to
and definitely what for

*

each pregnancy entombed, an oxblood cave of dream, ribbed
by maternal drum, venal, aortal, pulse threaded to origin's sorcery.

such exquisite visceral intimacy is our physical originality.
mother, harbouring outside, enfolds a life, vital

in its aspirations, mortal from the instant it's begun.
child, to grow among her machinery, her bodily thought

the electrical impulses of emotionality, the circulatory tides
which build, salted, at the uterine skin

storehouse for all that's to come.
in gestation's laboratory intricate each child schemed up

involuntary, and also into-dreamed.
how might this new one self?

what name to gird it to a destiny? should a stranger
ahead of their meeting be so depicted and loved!

*

clarity, diagnostic, to punch a livid scar,
scored in by World's cruel, never Child's,
endurable past the teat of infancy,
its chubby grips, past all the kingdoms of innocent
those shifting silvery downy dominions.

scores a hurt to perceive, alerted to this outlawry,
in the eyes of each parent
squadding forward the cherished one,
shielding, whether of two years
or of forty.

though most don't make it that far,
there are exceptions you know.
a gaze to conceal the twinning
of rarified sorrowed joys,

love shaken to the cosmic
because vulnerable

neuroward2east (for a.b.)

you go back or forward or simply out,
past a self's meniscus.
you have been where we have not.
what do you return
from death's tenderness?
for days you stayed only as breath
bonily, the leanest part,
shuttered behind the saw,
precise of the surgeon.
his hands at your skull
juggling the entrails
of all memory, fretting your life
for hours, a newborn thing
which nearly leaps
to break the thinnest rope
by which you span your spaces.

i sense you watch everything,
from in there, counting
across your palms still human,
days interleaving wrongly
with other days, the day
your brilliant blood flooded—
that which you adore,
what you would leave behind

unnamed

to get to where we need to go, there is a way, but one must be led there. at the appointed time, your guide will appear. usually these are of a celestial form, but there have been occasions, rare it is true, when this companion will take on a human guise; then, they will be of various forms but without variation, have a gaze whose radiance, fierce, is not of this world.

sometimes, the wily will track their way to this place, the place where we need to go, by shadowing the steps of another.

nonetheless, if you are wise, you will travel this long journey, to the mouth of the cave, only, by invitation, and, only, in the guardianship of this companion of whom we have already spoken. so, we will wait for them.

you ask, but how will we know this one has been appointed? how will we know that they are not, instead, an assassin assigned by the negative realms—whose cunning must not be under-estimated? and who, having taken us on a false route, will, at the earliest possible time, once we are far beyond this fortress's limits, turn while we rest? these are reasonable questions.

but for those who have learned the craft, to read at a glance the intention of another's force and will, this can be known; the constellation of their unearthly blood can be perceived, and in this, their origins.

yet i will acknowledge to you, it is fair that i acknowledge this to you, errors have been made in the past, and will be made again, on this matter of discernment—for the abilities of the negative ones, to replace truth with illusion, are also formidable. and the cost then is not only death to the deceived one, but also for any who travel with them.

the place we are going to is the land of our birth, the country of the henge, whose original race is half-mortal. you may have heard of them. they have been called, though they are not, druidic.

but it is accurate to augur that i have lived for an extended time, and that the end of my exile draws near. as the youngest of the three queens, it has not been the easiest of destinies. and, to you, my name cannot be known, though i ascended to one of the three stone chairs at twelve years old, though in fact i received the mantle when barely two. (mother, killed.) there, i was immersed in the arts and mysteries, never child, to harness and direct each of the powers, elemental; matrilineal succession, given to the female first-born of the three founding dynasties, this to balance the rights of each of the peoples.

so i wore a triple-horned crown, hewn from the sycamore tree we consider sacred—buried as ashes, before my departure.

once we reach the cave, it is through its caverns we must then go, descending rapidly into the earth's belly via steep corridors—these rocky ways are lit—before we reach the curtain that divides space's dimensions; where, time shimmers, it trembles; and, when we step through, the journey will begin as if anew. you will not forget who you are now, but you will hatch a different fate.

there is one other thing, which i cannot tell you, though i yearn to. i buried a staff made of crystal, before we departed. in its symbols, inscribed, are embedded all the seed-lights of our future, the old skills we will need to remember. the geographic co-ordinates of its hidden site are related to the henge, the room, and the sycamore—tattooed into my earthly and lighter minds. would that I could trust any of you with this information? but, if i am betrayed, my death is only the beginning of the price. you appreciate my caution (*pauses*). hush. the appointed one approaches.

untitled (once)

once, as a child
you stood
at the height
of mountains.
the sun, early
torched near
the arced
cloudless horizon.
flamed the snow
whose prisms blinked.
the silence, alpine
was absolute
it did not have
the fibrillations
of forest or ocean.
what made it
you had been bent
to call by the god-name.
but this presence
was of itself,
held to no mannish shape.
it guarded the mountains,
rivers, the lakes mirroring
below. a pact
it re-made with you.
and when you took
downwards... it brushed your
arm, as viscerally
as your lover's hand now does

II

prologue

the first time she understood,
properly, her powers
a storm had built
inside her house

doors were gutted, almost
thrown from hinges
by this wind unnatural
the photograph of a relative

flung across the room
in which she was
sitting, its glassface smashed

lay upwards; she had
been writing about this.

the pages of her poem
at 24 years old also flung
floating & dispersed
like tumbleweed playthings

it was not
her powers
that made this
event, poltergeisted,
she knew.
it was what
was opposing her,
truth's doom

untitled (witchly)

witchly,
we sluice
into this sudden
words. Self,
born anew,
like a stranger,
adjusts,
as an eyes' receptacles do,
to a darkened room.
Things, ideas, words
will take their shapes,
fix the borders
of names. Yet,
decades later,
you can still be turned mute
by world's errantry.
Humans, who
enact unholynesses.
How to relent on them.
Forgiveness has
her immediacy.
But will not hold
if, in the currents
swilling of time,
love be abraded

untitled (i want)

      nakedness

    to dress it

grabbing

thigh to cunt to eye

and gagged,

  speak my atrocity

I want a knife

  to feel it

your breast opening

my hands,

slitting across your face,

  their authority

i want your breath

  hot and finishing,

shaping some last syllable

death-weighted upon mine,

its coherence

    an audacity

amendment

You make me swoon

when roses make me think of you,

and what a waste

What the ground has got

is you,

and it should

We put you whole away, and it rained

to make you moss, i feel, to feather

your broken brain, to feed the seeds that grew

untitled (did i)

the human is avid
for the absolute

      but the runes do not lie.
      they say—

theory is not proof.
the hearth, wild, is not

      nor a heart, brumby
      its cultivated thing.

this love, animal
to swell, ill-secured

      by preference—maverick,
      private and uncivic

to buck
at any gift of vows.

      i didn't wear your diamond.
      i didn't curl

at the bowl of your milk.
i didn't ask

      for half the rent,
      though coinless.

i didn't.
did i tell you this?

untitled (recovery)

when you were first ill,
    febrile and viral,
looking out above the Harbour's glitter,
    its smash of watery mirrors,
you felt anchored

    by light's own shivering weight.
then, when the sun dropt
    into the water, Lorca,
of all Angels, came
    sat, solar

yet companionable,
    by your shaking self.
then you fevered for weeks

    but he had turned a thing
deep, and you had thought
    rotten, into benevolent life.
you wrote, to raise it.

    it is late, now.
the wind gathers, saults
    through the house
and a poet
is desperate enough, or not

Federico, i know that you remember
we should distrust, even
the language we wrestle
to purity, for what
it may still smuggle
over insidious borders

so the tyrants, also, dispatch
their execution orders,
the one for your name,
19th of august, 1936,
without the chill of doubt

untitled (On)

after a public reading by Beryl Langer and Rory Dufficy of Bertolt Brecht's poetry which included his 'On the Suicide of the Refugee W.B.'

suicide's frank
is to unbreathe alone—

no other to shepherd
that last refusal.

the absconding
of the body

torturable.
don't die yet. W.B. —

how many did you save?
the manuscript/s you hulked

by foot, over the mountains
frailed, to get to Portbou

in your suitcase, blacked.
pausing each every several

moments, so
you could still breathe.

it is said
the others left at Portbou

the following day,
they were allowed to cross

the French-Spanish border,
officials shocked

at the stature
of your passing

of that dimlylit threshold.
they say, a passable one.

be strong for the atrocity
you did. suicide

at its most
self-sovereignty.

untitled (the earth lugs on)

will have her peaceful hour,
endangered by and for us.

beasts, lulled to the knife, carbon's tock.
the self-congratulating fortunate,
the self-spawning rich

who slap off the beggar's welcome,
the boats, wasting, with their arrivals.
& across twenty-four hours

of newsprint
the platelets of children
will be sailing

on a Gazan beach,
through Ural airs.
these are old cries

renewed. for each breath
of faith, we will have
our possible weapon.

what isn't meant to happen,
and does. we revolve
on the delicate ankles of love.

untitled (when)

when i spoke again

it was of small places

what we survive in

with brusque eyes.

the earth which bites our bodies

is mouth, we call it earth

words are brief,

for what i dedicate without vocabulary

pollination

the bees are eating the honey. they nest in our minds,
    occasionally fleeing.
a single bee left mine by ear, only days ago.
it can be that quick: when the tongue is dumb, bees clot
    the mouth, making lips alive of them.

an old man runs for a tram in the street.
the whole thing chuckles with purpose, my being there,
    the taking risk.
the flowers have made a decision, too, collectively
    what season is.
they're crawling with blooming, ripping buds with purpose,
    which leaves hands out of it, though hands were there.
your face is sudden too:
there's an angel in each of us, seen in the comings, though
    the eyelids have a habit of closing at the crucial moment.
    i said, moment.
time is the biggest braggart of them all, settling finitude
    only to displace it.
it's begun again, and what do we have to hold it?

i'm blaming it on the bees. my mouth was loosened in a dream,
    and another one escaped.
they won't stop because of us. they're doing it now

untitled (time)

time is language
            mouth of elements
alluvial
bearing me here
      mouth of lava
whose vulcan transformations measure
me here

no words forgotten
           though the names clot
behind history, my tongue split
in so many directions
      i could not be understood or trusted

the storm

isn't really anything of the sort is it dear one not when you see the humble breath that lies gut-up underneath all that terrain of windfall, and the pearls gather their force within. of course i would be lying to pretend that this immensely glittering upheaval that broke our bonds was gentle, it's only that in the kinds of hands we're given nothing lies captured to speak of, not even the ash the daubs of pain we draw upon ourselves, well, let's not even speak of time its so many miracles. crystals refracting ceaseless frequencies, Empire furniture huddled like gilded fowl in the corners of Baroque mansions, vintage cars dawdling along the fat roads of countryside, the musselsoftness of a woman's innermost rising and falling with the till of a singular life, fossils small as postage-stamps that imprint epochs later on a suburban cove to be kept by the yowl of children i know, in whose presence upon my cheek I can feel their bloodwarmth, and space is so darkened where this immensity falls away, an oceanshelf abyss abutting an aquamarine shore, that i really don't feel privy to capture its perhaps more honest ways. anyhow, those in running shoes and others returning from the city-grid of a workers' rally drop their feet's great petals on the walk just beyond the windoworiel, powdering the wordkeep. yes! the government sucks! the morale of eating habits, the ding of fancy cars fishtailing, their dollardrum inhabitants, i know, i know, shhh. where we meet is a riverwash, not a tranquil reflective pond kept by fisherhusbands and the like, storing their trout for another dinner. ours the flow most peculiarly where the water rubbles, to be caught, tumbled by boulders, snags, then unloosed to drop away into straightasadie ribbons of light, that music. and you? now that the storm's settled its wager of rain and cloudedbright, we should be off. the trees are wintering bare. they hold urns of birds, just waiting for us, in this afterhush, to love one another i reckon

untitled (ahoy)

                         ahoy
unsilenced dead

all those shoals
too gentle
for the raised fists! of living

    *

all i want to do
tonight, is to be too fucked up

you can't change
what has happened, can, what will

    *

                this poem's getting all smashed up

    *

let

all those who are perpetrators / protectors
greed for the ether of valiums
to scintillate at 3 ams, body shuddering

let them in the volcanoes of ptsd
wonder how to breathe, to get to
dawn without self-death. the indignity
of a lifetime of meds   let

them.

    *

In the limed light
Of a single dawn you survive   ridescent, ruffian
breathed

    *

Prosecutorially—*are you sure*

    you just hadn't had too much to drink?

    your drink spiked! (legs faltered,
like a nobbled racehorse's.)
    are you sure

    *your father
    touched your breasts?*

    *

let them stub cigarettes

on the
inner of their wrists, mark

hatchetted their own bodies

                let them

*

                        (lull.)

*

let

me tell you, i wanted to tell you, *because i trust you*
about freud about incestuous abuse.
he rescinds his incendiary ideas

which had basically implied that the
almost entirely feminine of his clients were well, basically
being touched up as children by male relatives (or worse)

his assertions meet stun, derision,
freud reneges, turns actuals into *fantasy*.

it's all made up.

almost a century follows before scholarly, clinical re-adjustments—

*

*i wanted to tell you
and i trust you*

the moonlight has ethers, &

you have survived again, three months now, of almost mad.
self substructed to the essential. *are you with me?*

*

bared toothed blessings. plant seeds, seedlings, bulbs
that will corolla, heliotropic. that means
they lurch to light

all i want to do tonight is honour the dead who could not survive,
what others have survived, without explanation, honour all our dead

Note: this poem was written for and is dedicated to two beloved young ones without naming them.

Pls also see End-notes.

untitled (jump)

    jump from

        the mindwire.

            float,

  over

        demolition's

            debris.

  face

        shunting

            sunwards,

  in

        tearlogged's

            defiance

Catalogue

So:

naked, night after night. I was absolutely terrified.

the family.

 She seems satisfied.

There are other things I could add.

untitled (pacing)

      i am pacing daynight nightday thru
      the asylum of mind

re-read, notated highlighter neonyellow:

> *Haunting is a frightening experience. It always registers the harm inflicted or the loss sustained by a social violence done in the past or in the present. But haunting, unlike trauma, is distinctive for producing a something-to-be-done. Indeed, it seemed to me that haunting was precisely the domain of turmoil and trouble, that moment (of however long duration) when things are not in their assigned places, when the cracks and rigging are exposed, when the people who are meant to be invisible show up without any sign of leaving, when disturbed feelings cannot be put away, when something else, something different from before, seems like it must be done. – Avery F. Gordon*

H sd:
Drunk again?

Another h, sd: what you wrte, *hurt*

Examining, you took this to mean, do not spk further of vi'l'nces

      (you find out rand'om'y that someone is dying; you want to communicate; told, you can't)

See: ptsd arrows to irregulation arrows to 2 many bottle'o arrows to
yelling *hrt* too much truth

    by which you took, you, destabilising force. u, the unstable.
ion veering (discourteously)
out of orbit

    kp mth shut. Jst like they tell you. you shld.

I want to tell you a terrible thing. I am the ghost in the room; I am
the haunting who will not be done.

    Avery F. Gordon, p xvi, New Introduction, New Edition (2008), GHOSTLY
    MATTERS: Haunting and the Sociological Imagination *(University of Minnesota*
    Press, Minneapolis / London) The book was first published by the Press in 1997.

Canto 1

the conflict between the will to deny horrible events and the will to proclaim them aloud is the central dialectic of psychological trauma
— Judith Herman M. D.

destabilise.

the rocking-horse
canters
in the attic
the blue jewel of master's iris
scintillates, air-strikes
in a further century.
mothballs eat themselves

a little one climb
the gangly stairs
         knocks 3-times
as in all gruelling fairy-tales
on the oaken, hinge-aching door:
Let Me In!

flammable are the cities
where the children burn, searing
the solar upon the prisoner
being cuffed in

clawed, feline, clutch
to the hungry who will hunger; the raped
who will be raped again; the crone who sleeps
outside the bank, on pavement, in broad light
next to belongings' shoppingtrolley, to be safe

scimitar of beauty, fronds'
beauty as the seed toils to erupt
flowers? moist the waves that ever
rumble in, the littoral pocked
by shellshards, all begins, rottens

no, says the adamant child.

> *Quoted from the opening page of Herman's pioneering 1992 book,* Trauma and Recovery *(Basic Books, New York). The original poem was written ahead of reading her opening, which exemplifies both the power of the archetypal around 'haunting' and the fact her seminal work has well entered our world. The full opening is:*
>
> > THE ORDINARY RESPONSE TO ATROCITIES *is to banish them from consciousness. Certain violations of the social compact are too terrible to utter aloud: this is the meaning of the word* unspeakable. *Atrocities, however, refuse to be buried. Equally as powerful as the desire to deny atrocities is the conviction that denial does not work. Folk wisdom is filled with ghosts who refuse to rest in their graves until their stories are told. Murder will out. Remembering and telling the truth about terrible events are prerequisites both for the restoration of the social order and for the healing of individual victims.*
> >
> > *The conflict between the will to deny horrible events and the will to proclaim them aloud is the central dialectic of psychological trauma. People who have survived atrocities often tell their stories in a highly emotional, contradictory, and fragmented manner which undermines their credibility and thereby serves the twin imperatives of truth-telling and secrecy. When the truth is finally recognized, survivors can begin their recovery. But far too often secrecy prevails, and the story of the traumatic event surfaces not as a verbal narrative but as a symptom.*

untitled (nascent)

in the late, numinous hours
they always came.
this, loomed by
memory most nascent.
luminous shades,
larger than adults
and sometimes,
though these were infolded,
winged.
immoveable,
silent as statues,
yet with a ferociousness,
steely with their love,
descended, they stood
at the foot of your child bed

in the sea's

    green clarity, you tumble

        like a fish

        dripping sun

    later, you stand on hands

        barechested

    a child

        without questions

untitled (long)

go backwards
with all your hours
take them, who did no wrong

the flame blesses the ash
the hand, the departed mouth.
all things of love

praise the tree
leaning, horizonward

follow it, i said.
be stern with the patience

it is long that
the fruit and light take

to reach through wood

but from the moment
you began,
you have waited

End-notes

p1. ***untitled (Kill,)***: the betrayal is consequential, accidental, as he betrays her anti-Fascist intellectual spouse; I see the betrayal as total nonetheless as treachery can often murder collateral persons.

p27. ***prologue:*** a long time ago I read a classical poem referencing tumbleweed as playthings. I cannot source this idea now despite attempts to do so.

p34. ***untitled (On):*** thank-you so much to the readers acknowledged whose performances inspired this poem. W.B. refers to Walter Benjamin and 'torturable' and 'they say, a passable one' are both from Bertolt Brecht's poem, the latter referring to death's border.

p40. ***the storm:*** the title and first clause 'isn't really anything of the sort' are both *after* the opening of John Ashbery's *The Ice Storm*, a long prose-poem published by Hanuman Books (1987).

p42. ***untitled (ahoy):*** the repeat and use of 'let them' was central to the original poem, written mid-2023 and does not refer in any way to the 2025 book, *The Let Them Theory* (Mel Robbins).

The controversial explorations of Freud's reneging on his original seduction theory are central to a number of also pioneering writers, and remains debated in contemporary theory. Chief among these authors with seminal volumes are: Alice Miller's *Thou Shalt Not Be Aware* (published first in Germany in 1981; a paperback English edition was published by Hunter Hannum in 1998, translated by Hildegarde Hannum) and Jeffrey Moussaieff Masson's *The Assault on Truth: Freud's Suppression of the Seduction Theory* (Farrar, Straus and Giroux, 1984).

Acknowledgements

Due to the number of extraordinary Australian poets and literary associates with whom I have engaged over the time I have written and published in this artform, I will not name you all, but I will impart my thanks personally as I can. An especial Thank-you must be made to: my most loved daughters three who have been instrumental in my undertaking of this book, and pricelessly, often in its critical hours, and those peaks of anxiety and distress; Robert, my Beloved, as always; Simon Ryan; Jennifer Nguyen; George Kartas; Autumn Royal; Tim Loveday; Sophie Gaur, for your humaneness combined with designer genius; David Musgrave, for full creative freedom; and Ann Vickery, for those crucial, incisive late mss discussions.

Though I remain in permanent disconnection from my direct birth-family I insist on sending love to my six brothers. Jules, I love you.

Finally, a number of these poems have been published in present or earlier versions in journals and other publications. I say Thank-you to all the editors, staff and funders who made these outcomes possible.

Bio

Jacinta Le Plastrier is a Melbourne/Naarm-based writer, poet, essayist, editor and publisher. Her writing, journalism, criticism and poetry have appeared in anthologies by Oxford University Press, Penguin Books, Pan Picador and Melbourne University Press, along with *The Guardian, The Age, Sydney Morning Herald, Australian Book Review, ABC 24 Hours, The Wheeler Centre (Hot Desk Fellowship), sick leave journal, Cordite* and *Meanjin*, among others. She is the former Chief Executive at the national poetry body, Australian Poetry, where she also sat as Publisher. This role included the co-founding of the *Best of Australian Poems* annual series with Toby Fitch and Ellen van Neerven. Jacinta also has a private practice of writing and teaching on the supernatural.

www.ingramcontent.com/pod-product-compliance
Lightning Source LLC
Chambersburg PA
CBHW020217090426
42734CB00008B/1114